CAMBRIDGE
UNIVERSITY PRESS

CAMBRIDGE ENGLISH
Language Assessment
Part of the University of Cambridge

CAMBRIDGE
OFFICIAL
PREPARATION MATERIAL

Kid's Box

Updated
Second Edition

T0372620

**Workbook 1**
with Online Resources

American English

**Caroline Nixon & Michael Tomlinson**

**Cambridge University Press**
www.cambridge.org/elt

**Cambridge Assessment English**
www.cambridgeenglish.org

Information on this title: www.cambridge.org/ 9781316627167

© Cambridge University Press & Assessment 2008, 2015, 2017

This publication is in copyright. Subject to statutory exception
and to the provisions of relevant collective licensing agreements,
no reproduction of any part may take place without the written
permission of Cambridge University Press.

First published 2008
Second edition 2015
Updated second edition 2016

20  19  18  17

Printed in Italy by L.E.G.O. S.p.A.

*A catalogue record for this publication is available from the British Library*

ISBN  978-1-316-62716-7  Workbook with Online Resources 1
ISBN  978-1-316-62750-1  Student's Book 1
ISBN  978-1-316-62700-6  Teacher's Book 1
ISBN  978-1-316-62719-8  Class Audio CDs 1 (4 CDs)
ISBN  978-1-316-62733-4  Teacher's Resource Book with Online Audio 1
ISBN  978-1-316-62575-0  Flashcards 1
ISBN  978-1-316-62785-3  Interactive DVD with Teacher's Booklet 1 (PAL/NTSC)
ISBN  978-1-316-62706-8  Presentation Plus 1
ISBN  978-1-316-63015-0  Posters 1
ISBN  978-1-316-62698-6  Monty's Alphabet Book Levels 1–2

Additional resources for this publication at www.cambridge.org/elt/kidsboxamericanenglish

Cambridge University Press has no responsibility for the persistence or accuracy
of URLs for external or third-party internet websites referred to in this publication,
and does not guarantee that any content on such websites is, or will remain,
accurate or appropriate. Information regarding prices, travel schedules, and other
factual information given in this work is correct at the time of first printing but
Cambridge University Press does not guarantee the accuracy of such information
thereafter.

# Kid's Box

American English

## Workbook 1

Caroline Nixon & Michael Tomlinson

**1** **Hi!** 4

**2** **My school** 10

Marie's math – Adding 16

Trevor's values – Make friends 17

**3** **Favorite toys** 18

**4** **My family** 24

Marie's art – Mixing colors 30

Trevor's values – Be kind 31

**Review 1 2 3 4** 32

**5** **Our pets** 34

**6** **My face** 40

Marie's science – The senses 46

Trevor's values – Take care of pets 47

**7** **Wild animals** 48

**8** **My clothes** 54

Marie's geography – Habitats 60

Trevor's values – Love nature 61

**Review 5 6 7 8** 62

**9** **Fun time!** 64

**10** **At the amusement park** 70

Marie's sports – Things for sports 76

Trevor's values – Work in teams 77

**11** **Our house** 78

**12** **Party time!** 84

Marie's art – Fruit in paintings 90

Trevor's values – Keep clean 91

**Review 9 10 11 12** 92

Grammar reference 94

Language Portfolio 98

# 1 Hi!

**1** ✏️ Match.

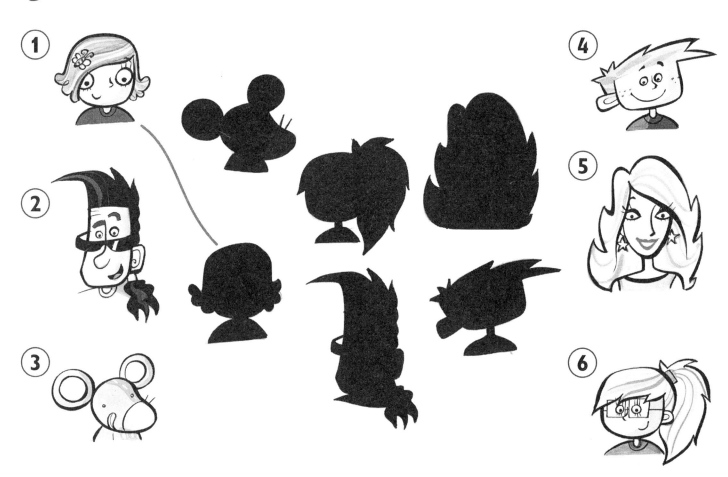

**2** 🔊 CD1 ✏️ Listen and circle the ✔ or ✗.

1  ☑ ✔  ☐ ✗     2  ☐ ✔  ☐ ✗     3  ☐ ✔  ☐ ✗     4  ☐ ✔  ☐ ✗

**3** 🔍✏️ Look and match.

**4** ✏️ Connect the dots.

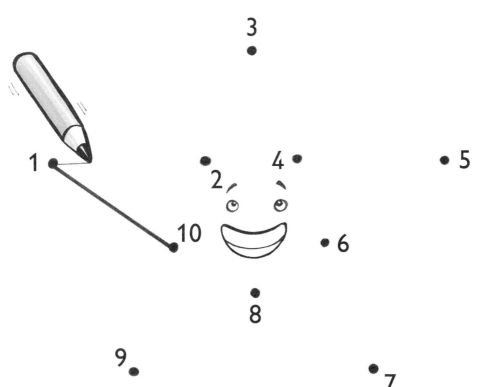

## 5 ▶9 CD1 ✏ Listen and write the number.

(1) 6

(2) ☐

(3) ☐

(4) ☐

(5) ☐

(6) ☐

## 6 ✏ Draw and write.

Me!

I'm _____ Sally _____ .

I'm _____ seven _____ .

Me!

I'm _____ .

I'm _____ .

Listen and color.

**8** 15 CD1 🖉 Listen and circle the "s" words.

**9** 16 CD1 🖉 Listen and check (✓) the box.

# My picture dictionary

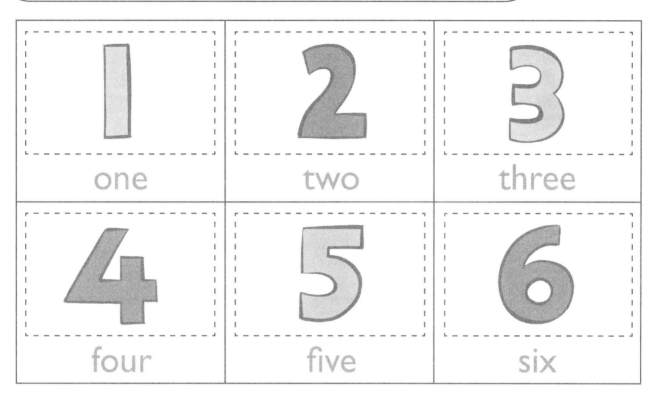

one

two

three

four

five

six

# My star card

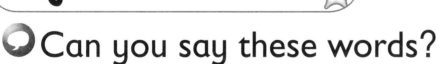
Can you say these words?

Color the stars.

**1** 🔊 21 CD1 ✏️ Listen and color.

**2** ✏️ Draw your table.

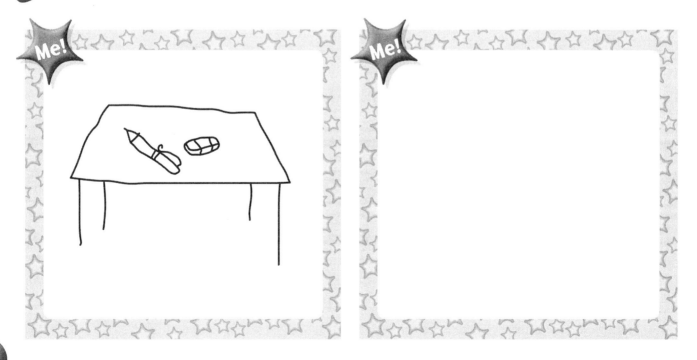

**3** 🖊 Draw three pictures.

🗨🖊 Now tell your friend.
Draw your friend's pictures.

Number one is a chair.

**4** 🖊 Count. Write the number.

**5** 📀 26 CD1 ✏️ Listen and write the number.

**6** ✏️ 💬 Match and answer.

**7** 🔍✏️ Look and read. Check (✓) or put an ✗.

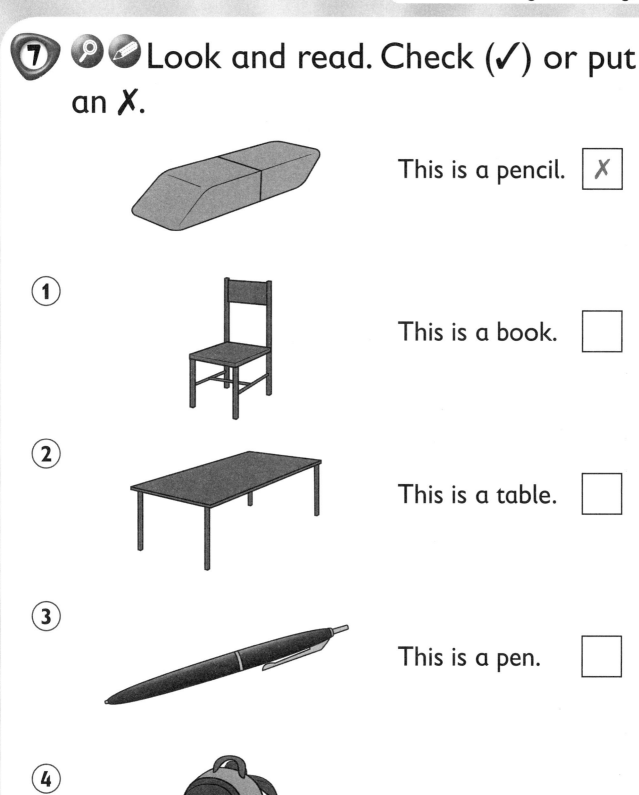

This is a pencil. ✗

**1** This is a book. ☐

**2** This is a table. ☐

**3** This is a pen. ☐

**4** This is a bag. ☐

**8** 🔊30 ✏️ Listen. Color the "p" words pink. Color the "b" words blue.

**9** 🔊31 ✏️ Listen and color.

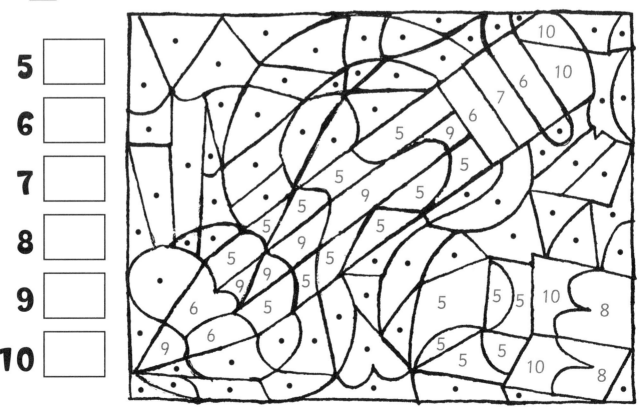

5
6
7
8
9
10

# My picture dictionary

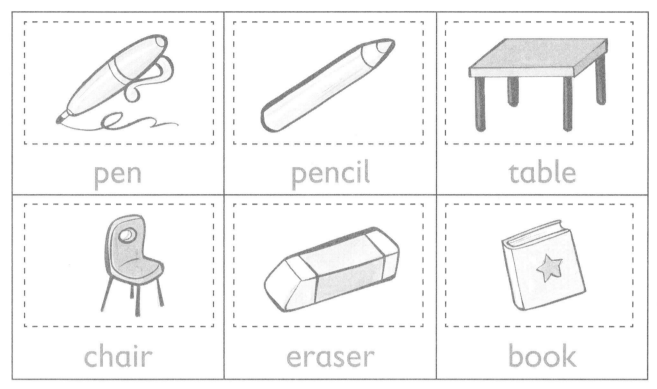

pen

pencil

table

chair

eraser

book

# My star card

 Can you say these words?

Color the stars.

Now you! **1**  Write the numbers.

① 1 + 4 = _5_     ② 4 + 1 = ____

③ 3 + 2 = ____     ④ 2 + 3 = ____

⑤ 4 + 3 = ____     ⑥ 3 + 4 = ____

**2** Write and answer. Say.

① _3_ + _2_ = _5_

② ____ + ____ = ____

③ ____ + ____ = ____

④ ____ + ____ = ____

What are three and two?

Five.

**3** 💬✏️ Ask two friends and write.
Then draw and color.

What's your name?    How old are you?

I'm ____Sam____ .
I'm ___seven___ .

I'm _____ .
I'm _____ .

I'm _____ .
I'm _____ .

**1** 38 CD1 ✏ Listen and circle the ✓ or ✗.

①  ✓ ✗   ② 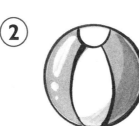 ✓ ✗   ③  ✓ ✗

④  ✓ ✗   ⑤  ✓ ✗   ⑥  ✓ ✗

**2** 🔍 ✏ Look and complete.

①      ?

②      ?

③      ?

④      ?

**3**  **41** **CD1** Listen and draw colored lines.

**4** Color the toys.

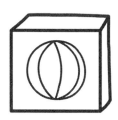   

Now ask and answer. Color your friend's toys.

What color's your ball?     It's white.

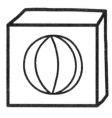   

# 5 ⟩ 🔊 44 CD1 ✏️ Listen and write the number.

# 6 ⟩ 🔍 ✏️ Look and circle.

Listen and draw lines.

Matt      Alice      Hugo

Eva      Mark      Mary

**8** **49** CD1 ✏️ Listen and circle "t" or "d."

① **t** d

② t d

③ t d

④ t d

⑤ t d

⑥ t d

⑦ t d

⑧ t d

**9** **50** CD1 ✏️ Listen and color.

# My picture dictionary

| | | |
|---|---|---|
| car | ball | bike |
| train | doll | computer |

# My star card

 Can you say these words?

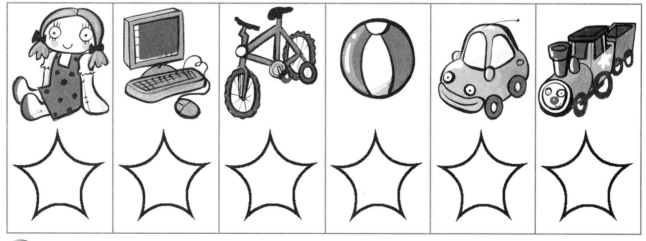

Color the stars.

# 4 My family

**1** 💬 ✏️ **Who is it? Match and answer.**

**2** ▶️ ✏️ **Listen and color.**

**CD2**

This is
my family.

**3**  Listen and draw colored lines.

**4** Draw your family.

Me!

**5** 🔊 10 CD2 ✏️ Listen and color the stars.

This is my family.

**6** ✏️ 💬 Circle and say.

She's beautiful.

**7**  Look and complete the words.

<u>b</u> eautiful

①
___ld

o d l

②
___ad

d s a

③
___gly

u l y g

④
___appy

p p h a y

⑤
___oung

u n y o g

## 8. 🔊 16 CD2 ✏️ Listen and circle the "a" in the words.

**1** c a t

**2** s a d

**3** b a g

**4** h a p p y

**5** f a m i l y

**6** b l a c k

## 9. 🔊 17 CD2 ✏️ Listen and write the number.

# My picture dictionary

grandfather    grandmother    mother

father    brother    sister

# My star card

Can you say these words?

Color the stars.

Read and color. Write.

| g | r | e | e | n |

| o | r | a | n | g | e |

| p | u | r | p | l | e |

| p | i | n | k |

| ~~g~~ | ~~r~~ | ~~a~~ | ~~y~~ |

1 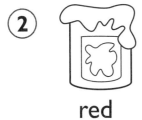 white +  black =   | g | r | a | y |

2  red + yellow... red + white =  ☐ ☐ ☐ ☐

3  blue +  yellow = ☐ ☐ ☐ ☐ ☐ ☐

4  red + yellow = ☐ ☐ ☐ ☐ ☐ ☐

5 blue + red = ☐ ☐ ☐ ☐ ☐ ☐

**2** 🔍✏️ Draw and complete the pictures.

# Review

**1** 🔊 ✏️ Listen and connect the dots.

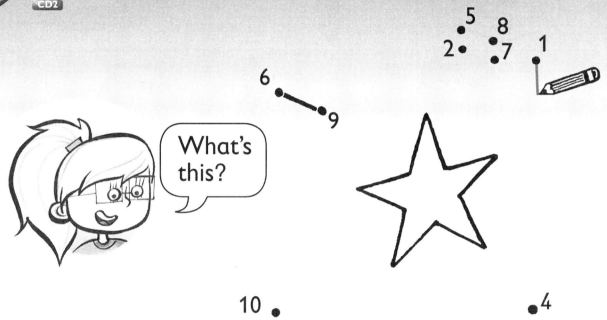

What's this?

**2** 🔍 ✏️ Look and draw.

**3** 🔍✏️ Count and write the number.

| | | | | | |
|---|---|---|---|---|---|
| 6 | [ ] | [ ] | [ ] | [ ] | [ ] |

**4** 💬🔍 Say, look, and answer.

Two, pencil.　　He's ugly!

① ② ③ ④ ⑤

# 5 Our pets

**1** 🔘 28 CD2 ✏️ **Listen and circle the ✔ or ✗.**

**2** 🔍 ✏️ **Look and write the words.**

| a bird | a cat | a dog | a fish | a horse | ~~a mouse~~ |

① _a mouse_

② _____

③ _____

④ _____

⑤ _____

⑥ _____

**3** 🖊️ Color the pets.

🗨️🖊️ Now ask and answer. Color your friend's pets.

What color is the fish?  It's blue.

**4** 🗨️🖊️ Read and answer.

| birds | fish | ~~mice~~ | cats | horses |
|-------|------|----------|------|--------|

1 What are they? They're _ _ _ _ _ _ _ _ _ _ _ _ _ _ _ _ .

2 What are they? They're _ _ _ _ _ _ _ _ _ _ _ _ _ _ _ _ .

3 What are they? They're _ _ _ _ _ mice _ _ _ _ _ .

4 What are they? They're _ _ _ _ _ _ _ _ _ _ _ _ _ _ _ _ .

5 What are they? They're _ _ _ _ _ _ _ _ _ _ _ _ _ _ _ _ .

## 5 🔍✏️ Read and circle.

1. short / (long)
2. clean / dirty
3. small / big
4. short / long
5. big / small
6. clean / dirty

## 6 🔊33 CD2 ✏️ Listen and follow.

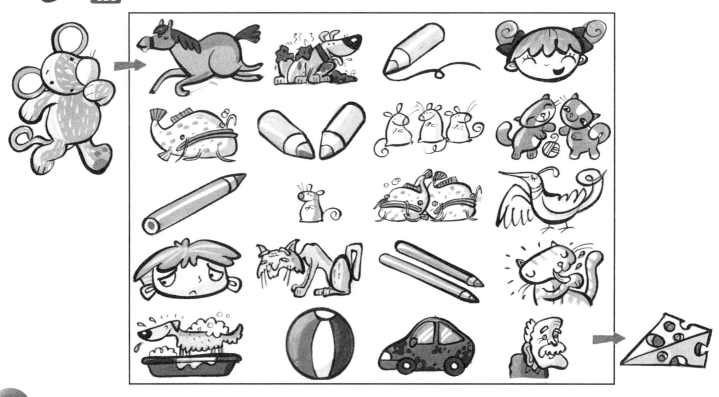

**7** 🔍✏️Look and read. Check (✓) or put an ✗.

This is a horse. ✓

(1)

This is a bird. ☐

(2)

This is a mouse. ☐

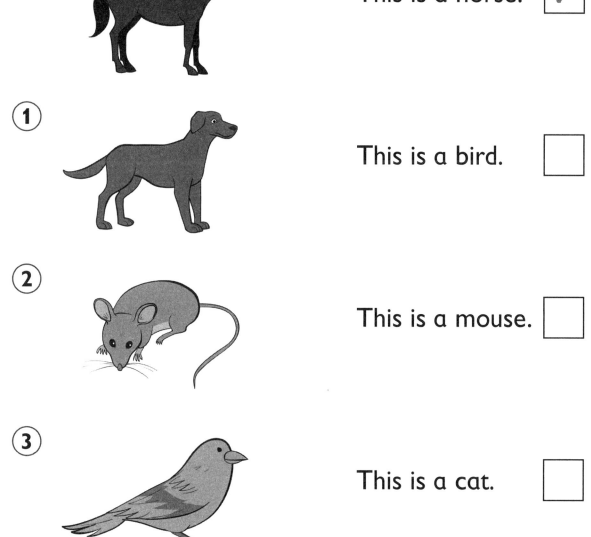

(3)

This is a cat. ☐

(4)

This is a fish. ☐

## 8 🎵 ✏️ Listen and write "a" or "e."

1. p_e_ts
2. b__g
3. c__t
4. p__n
5. t__n
6. s__d
7. S__lly
8. h__ppy

## 9 🔍 ✏️ Read and write the number.

| a dirty dog | 3 | a big dog | ☐ | two short dogs | ☐ |
| a long dog | ☐ | three small dogs | ☐ | a clean dog | ☐ |

## My picture dictionary

dog

bird

cat

fish

mouse

horse

## My star card

Can you say these words?

Color the stars.

## 1 🎵42 CD2 ✏️ Listen and draw colored lines.

① ② ③ ④ ⑤ ⑥

## 2 ✏️ Circle the different word.

| | | | | |
|---|---|---|---|---|
| ① | bike | nose | train | doll |
| ② | table | horse | mouse | bird |
| ③ | eyes | ears | teeth | ball |
| ④ | book | pen | car | pencil |
| ⑤ | fish | horse | cat | head |
| ⑥ | dog | four | ten | seven |

**3** 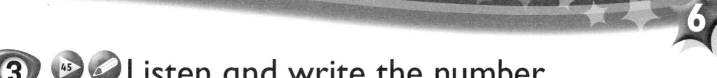 **45 CD2** Listen and write the number.

□  □  1

□  □  □

**4** Write the words.

e a r s    e y e s    h a i r    m o u t h

n o s e    t e e t h

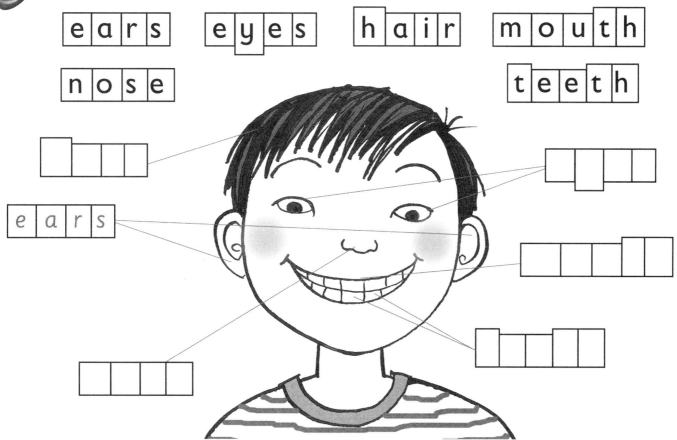

e a r s

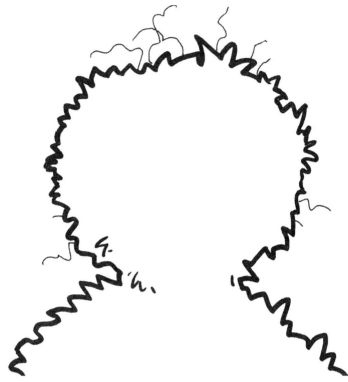

**6** Draw your face and write.

Me!

| blue |
| brown |
| green |
| big |
| small |
| short |
| long |

I have _____ eyes.

I have a _____ mouth.

I have _____ hair.

**7** Read and write.

**A monster**

I'm a happy monster. My ___head___ is very big. I have long

black (1) _____ . I have three (2) _____ .

On my face, my (3) _____ is small, but I don't have

a small mouth. In my mouth, I have big (4) _____ .

I have a pet. My pet is a (5) _____ .

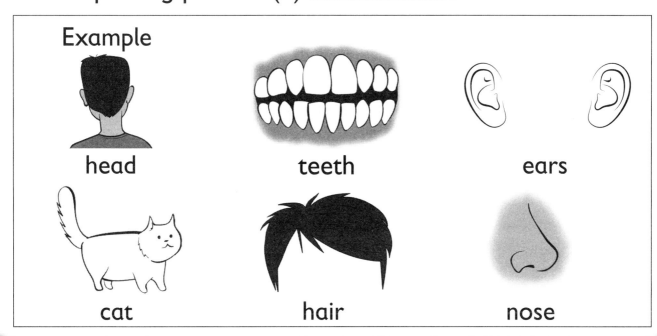

Example

head          teeth          ears

cat          hair          nose

**8** 🔊 52 CD2 ✏️ Listen and complete the words.

1. f r og

2. ___ ___ own

3. ___ ___ aw

4. ___ ___ een

5. ___ ___ other

6. ___ ___ ain

**9** 🔊 53 CD2 ✏️ Listen, look, and draw. Write.

~~eye~~   hair   mouth   nose

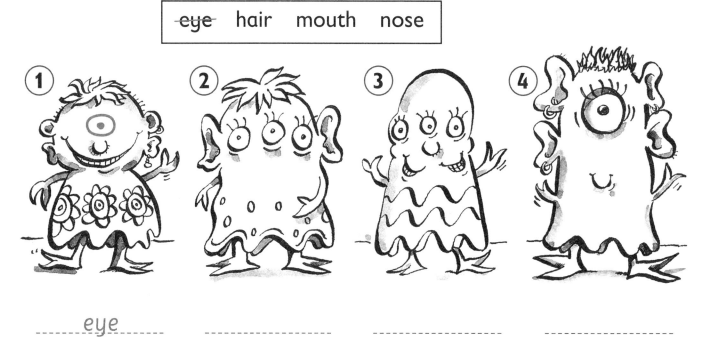

1   2   3   4

___ eye ___     _____     _____     _____

44

## My picture dictionary

ears    eyes    mouth

nose    hair    teeth

## My star card

Can you say these words?

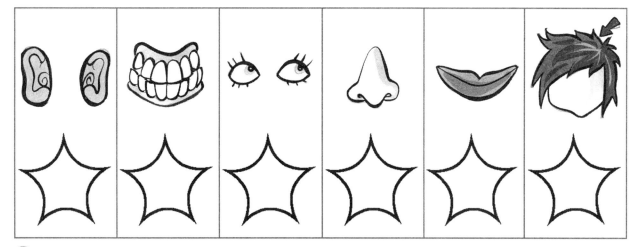

Color the stars.

**1** Look and write. Find and draw.

**1**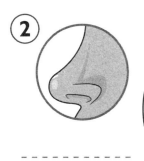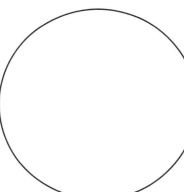

hear

| taste |
| touch |
| ~~hear~~ |
| see |
| smell |

**2**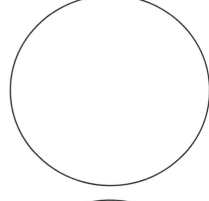

**3**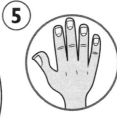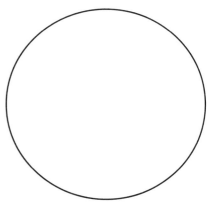

**4**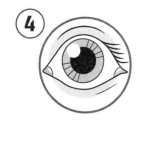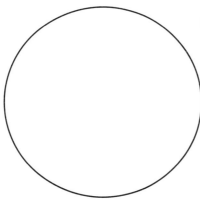

**5**

**2** Point and say.

What can you smell?

Flowers.

**3** 🔍✏️ **Read and match.**

①

②

I brush my cat.

I wash my horse.

I feed my fish.

I walk my dog.

③

④

**4** 🔍✏️ **Draw and write.**

Me!

This is my _____ . I _____
and _____ my _____ .

| brush |
| feed |
| wash |
| walk |

# 7 Wild animals

**1** 🔊 ✏️ **Listen and connect the dots.**

**2** ✏️ **Read and draw lines.** ↓ ↘ →

**①**

| doll | bike | ball |
|------|------|------|
| nine | hippo | bag |
| table | seven | eight |

**②**

| elephant | ten | crocodile |
|----------|-----|-----------|
| chair | seven | car |
| computer | five | bag |

**③**

| pencil | ball | bag |
|--------|------|-----|
| tiger | eraser | one |
| doll | five | book |

**④**

| bike | two | door |
|------|-----|------|
| three | doll | train |
| snake | monkey | giraffe |

## 7

**3** 🔍✏️ Read and answer. Write "yes" or "no."

1️⃣ Are the giraffes sad? _no_

2️⃣ Are the elephants happy? _____

3️⃣ Are the crocodiles long? _____

4️⃣ Are the snakes short? _____

**4** ✏️ Color the animals.

💬✏️ Now ask and answer. Color your friend's animals.

My giraffes are purple.

**5** **9** CD3 ✎ Listen and write the number.

**6** 🔍 ✎ Read and check (✓) or put an ✗.

| Animals | hands | arms | legs | feet | tails |
|---|---|---|---|---|---|
| snakes | ✗ | ✗ | ✗ | ✗ | ✓ |
| monkeys | | | | | |
| birds | | | | | |
| elephants | | | | | |
| crocodiles | | | | | |
| fish | | | | | |
| tigers | | | | | |
| zebras | | | | | |

**7** 🔍✏️ Look and read. Write "yes" or "no."

The elephants have small ears.          no

① The monkeys are on bikes.          ﹍﹍﹍﹍

② The giraffes are under the elephants.          ﹍﹍﹍﹍

③ The small giraffe is fat.          ﹍﹍﹍﹍

④ The tigers are next to the crocodiles.          ﹍﹍﹍﹍

⑤ The snakes have eyes.          ﹍﹍﹍﹍

**8** 🔊13 CD3 ✏️ Listen and write "a," "e," or "i."

① l e g

② f__sh

③ bl__ck

④ b__g

⑤ h__ppo

⑥ p__n

⑦ s__ster

⑧ h__nd

**9** ✏️ Draw and write.

Me!

My favorite wild animals are _____ .
They're _____ .
They have _____ .

# My picture dictionary

| crocodile | elephant | tiger |
|---|---|---|
| hippo | giraffe | snake |

# My star card

 Can you say these words?

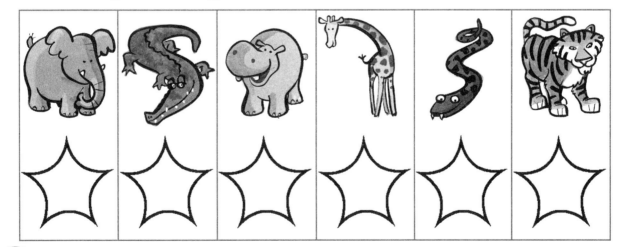

Color the stars.

# 8 My clothes

**1** 🔍 ✏️ Find and circle the number.

| | | | | | | | | | | |
|---|---|---|---|---|---|---|---|---|---|---|
| 🧦 | 1 | 2 | 3 | 4 | 5 | 6 | 7 | 8 | 9 | (10) |
| 👕 | 1 | 2 | 3 | 4 | 5 | 6 | 7 | 8 | 9 | 10 |
| 👗 | 1 | 2 | 3 | 4 | 5 | 6 | 7 | 8 | 9 | 10 |
| 👟 | 1 | 2 | 3 | 4 | 5 | 6 | 7 | 8 | 9 | 10 |
| 🧥 | 1 | 2 | 3 | 4 | 5 | 6 | 7 | 8 | 9 | 10 |
| 👖 | 1 | 2 | 3 | 4 | 5 | 6 | 7 | 8 | 9 | 10 |

**2** 🔊 17 CD3 💬 Listen and answer.

**3**  **Listen and color.**

**4** **Draw and write.**

Me!

My favorite clothes are my _____ .

**5** 🔊 23 CD3 ✏️ Listen and color.

Sue

Nick

Kim

Tony

May

**6** 🔊 24 CD3 ✏️ Listen and match.

**7** Read the question. Listen and write a name or a number. There are two examples.

3   ~~Kim~~   Tom   ~~10~~   8   Bill   9

What is the name of the girl? _____ Kim _____

How old is she? _____ 10 _____

① What is the name of the dog? _____

② How old is the dog? _____

③ What is the name of Kim's brother? _____

④ How old is Kim's brother? _____

⑤ How many children are in Kim's class? _____

# 8 Listen and write "a," "e," "i," or "o."

1. d_o_ll

2. c___p

3. d___g

4. p___n

5. f___sh

6. s___ck

7. b___x

8. s___x

# 9 Write the sentences.

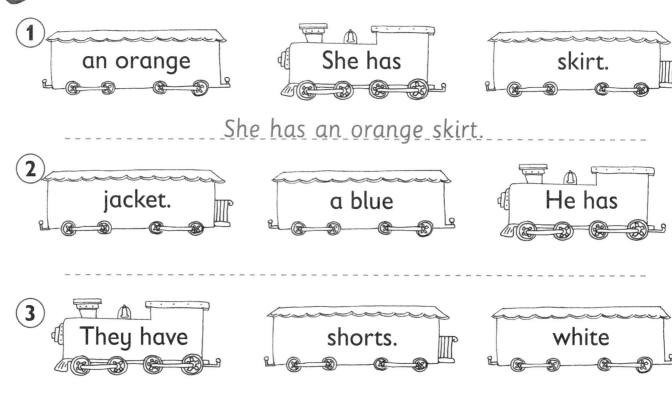

1. an orange | She has | skirt.

She has an orange skirt.

2. jacket. | a blue | He has

3. They have | shorts. | white

# My picture dictionary

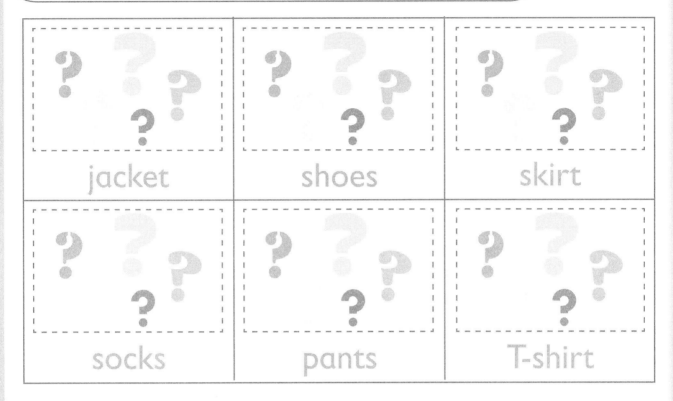

jacket

shoes

skirt

socks

pants

T-shirt

# My star card

 Can you say these words?

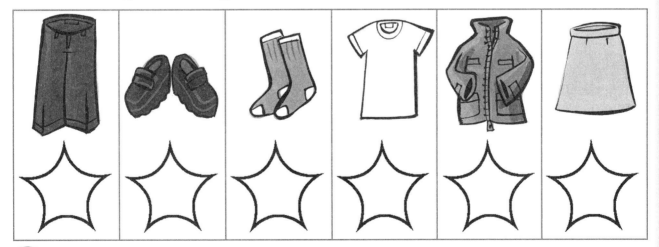

Color the stars.

**1**  Read and check (✓) or put an X.

|  | river | plain | forest |
|---|---|---|---|
| fish | ✓ | X | X |
| giraffe | | | |
| hippo | | | |
| crocodile | | | |

Now you! **2**  Read. Write and draw.

| plains | long | gray | elephant | forests |

This animal is from

____plains____ and

_____ . It's big

and _____ .

It has two big

ears and a very

_____ nose.

What is it? It's an

_____ .

**3** 🖊 Read and write the number.

① The birds are sad. `4`

② The river is dirty. ☐

③ The forest has trees. ☐

④ The river doesn't have fish. ☐

⑤ The forest doesn't have trees. ☐

⑥ The birds are happy. ☐

⑦ The river has fish. ☐

⑧ The river is clean. ☐

# Review

**1** 🔍 ✏️ Read, draw, and color.

**Bill**
long shoes
a dirty T-shirt
a big nose
a sad mouth
purple pants

**Ben**
short shoes
a happy mouth
green hair
a small nose
a red jacket

**2** 🔊37 CD3 💬 Listen and say "Bill" or "Ben."

**3** 💬 Say the sentences.

Fish and snakes don't have legs.

| | | | | |
|---|---|---|---|---|
|  | and |  | no legs. | |
|  | and |  | no hands. | |
|  | and |  | no arms. | |
|  | and |  | no hair. | |

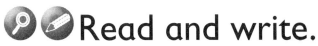 # Read and write.

arms    ears    ~~face~~    hands    mouth    tail    two    two

## At the safari park

I'm small and brown. I have a funny ① _____ *face* _____

**2**

with ② _____ big ③ _____ and a big

④ _____ . My ⑤ _____ are long and

**2**

I have ⑥ _____

big ⑦ _____ . I have

a long ⑧ _____ .

# 9 Fun time!

**1** 🔊 ✏️ **Listen and write the number.**

**2** 🔍 ✏️ **Read and match.**

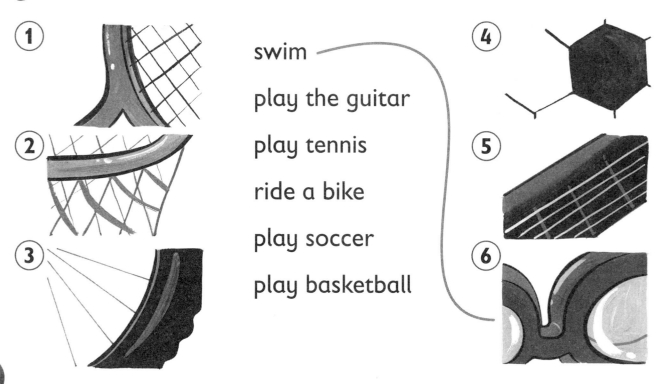

1

2

3

swim

play the guitar

play tennis

ride a bike

play soccer

play basketball

4

5

6

## 3 🔍✏️ Find six words.

① 

| w | a | s | g | r | i | d | e |
|---|---|---|---|---|---|---|---|
| r | s | p | u | g | i | t | a |
| a | w | b | i | k | e | r | p |
| t | i | n | t | i | s | l | l |
| o | m | l | a | s | t | c | a |
| o | m | e | r | x | u | r | y |
| t | e | n | n | i | s | a | e |

? a ?

③

?

②

? ?

④

play the ?

## 4 ✏️ Write the words.

①  ②  ③  ④  ⑤  ⑥

soccer ~~guitar~~ play ride swim tennis

① play the _guitar_

② _____ basketball

③ play _____

④ play _____

⑤ _____ a bike

⑥ _____

**5** 🔊 46 CD3 ✏️ Listen and check (✓) or put an **X**.

① ☒   ② ☐   ③ ☐

④ ☐   ⑤ ☐   ⑥ ☐

**6** ✏️ What can you do? Draw and write.

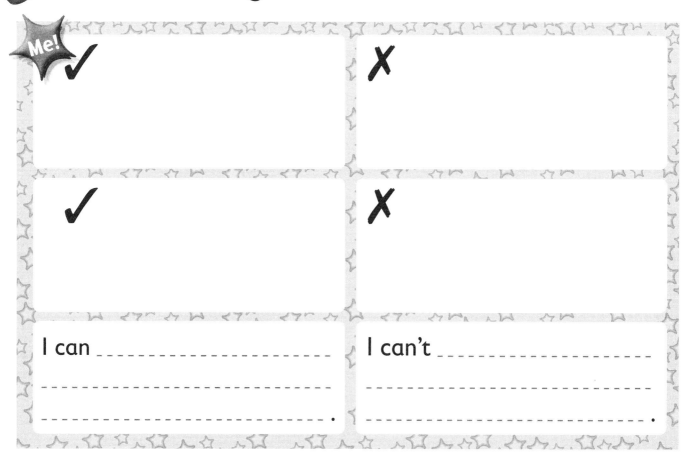

Me! ✓

✗

✓

✗

I can _____ .

I can't _____ .

7 Look and write the words.

Example

b a s k e t b a l l

b s k a t e
b l l a

Questions

1

_ _ _

r c a

2

_ _ _ _

k i b e

3

_ _ _ _ _

r s h o e

4

_ _ _ _ _ _

n i n e t s

5

_ _ _ _ _ _

t a g u i r

## 8 🔊50 CD3 ✏️ Listen and circle "l" in the words.

①

Lily

② blue

③ soccer ball

④ pencil

⑤ play

⑥ clean

⑦ yellow

⑧ plane

## 9 ✏️ Write the words.

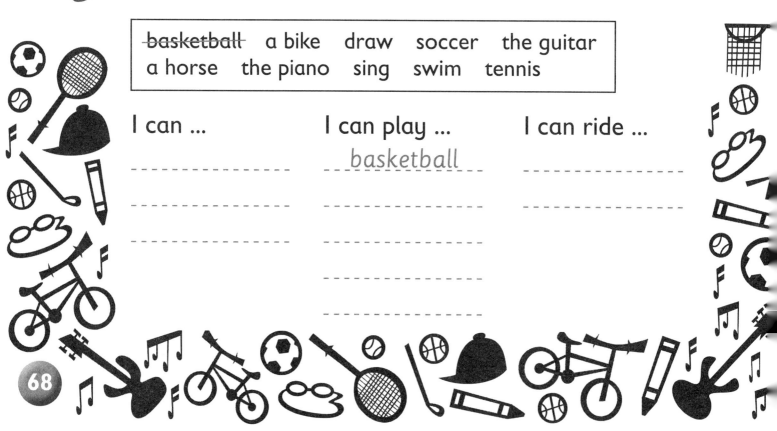

| basketball a bike draw soccer the guitar |
| a horse the piano sing swim tennis |

I can ...

_____
_____
_____

I can play ...
basketball
_____
_____
_____

I can ride ...

_____
_____

## My picture dictionary ✩✩

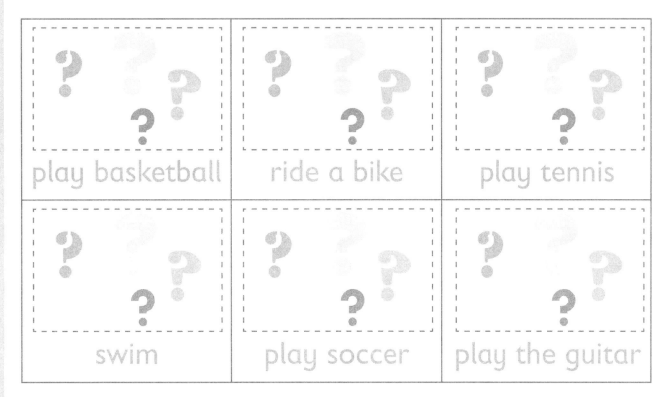

| | | |
|---|---|---|
| play basketball | ride a bike | play tennis |
| swim | play soccer | play the guitar |

## My star card ✩✩

 Can you say these words?

Color the stars.

# 10 At the amusement park

**1** ✏️ Write the words.

> bike   boat   bus   car   ~~helicopter~~
> truck   motorcycle   plane   train

**⑤**

**①**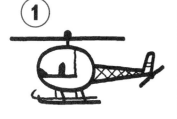

**②**

**③**

**④**

Crossword:

- 1 down: h e l i c o p t e r
- 2 across
- 3 across
- 4 down
- 5 across
- 6 across
- 7 across (with 8 down)
- 9 across

**⑥**

**⑦**

**⑧**

**⑨**

**2** 🔊 CD4 ✏️ Listen and color.

**3** Draw stars.

Now ask and answer. Draw your friend's stars.

 Where's the star?

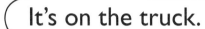 It's on the truck.

   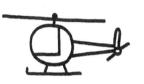

**4** Write the words.

truck   T-shirt   helicopter   boat   pants   plane
skirt   jacket   shoes   motorcycle   socks   bus

truck

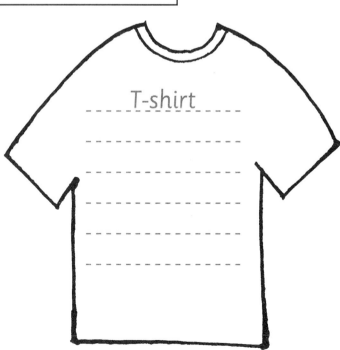
T-shirt

## 5 Listen and draw colored lines.

## 6 Draw and write.

| riding | horse | bike | motorcycle | driving | sitting |
| truck | bus | ship | flying | plane | helicopter |

Me!

I'm _____ a _____ .

**7** Listen and check (✓) the box.
There is one example.

Where's the truck?

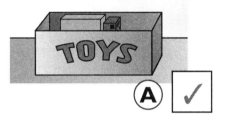 **A** ✓   **B** ☐   **C** ☐

**1** What's Anna doing?

 **A** ☐   **B** ☐   **C** ☐

**2** Which toy is under the chair?

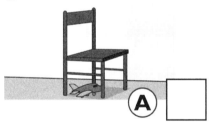 **A** ☐  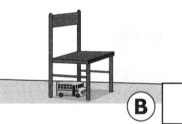 **B** ☐   **C** ☐

**3** What color is Matt's motorcycle?

 **A** ☐   **B** ☐    **C** ☐

**4** Which boy is Alex?

  **A** ☐   **B** ☐    **C** ☐

**8** 🎧 CD4 ✏️ Listen and write "a," "e," "i," "o," or "u."

1. h_a_ppy
2. s___cks
3. b___s
4. s___ng
5. d___ck
6. f___sh
7. s___d
8. l___g

**9** 🔍 ✏️ Read and complete.

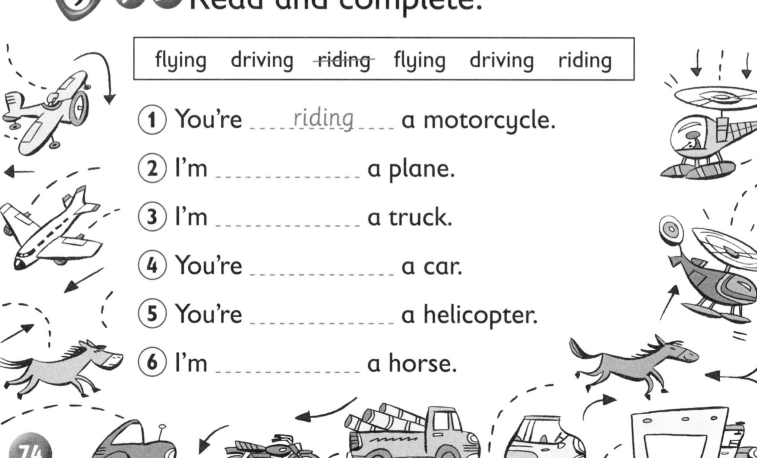

| flying | driving | ~~riding~~ | flying | driving | riding |

1. You're ____riding____ a motorcycle.
2. I'm _____ a plane.
3. I'm _____ a truck.
4. You're _____ a car.
5. You're _____ a helicopter.
6. I'm _____ a horse.

## My picture dictionary

bus

truck

motorcycle

helicopter

plane

boat

## My star card

Can you say these words?

Color the stars.

**Now you! 1**  Match and say.

She has a big ball.

①    ②    ③    ④    ⑤

bike | big ball | small ball | boat | horse

**2**   Match and write.

horse   boat   basketball   ~~bike~~   Ping-Pong

① They're riding a _____bike_____ .

② They're sitting on a _____ .

③ They're playing _____ .

④ They're playing _____ .

⑤ They're riding a _____ .

**3** 💬 ✏️ Work in teams. Color the boxes.

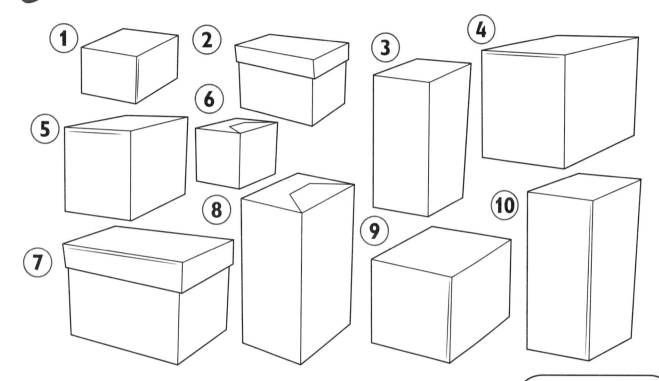

**4** 🤸 ✏️ Play the game in teams.

Number one is yellow.

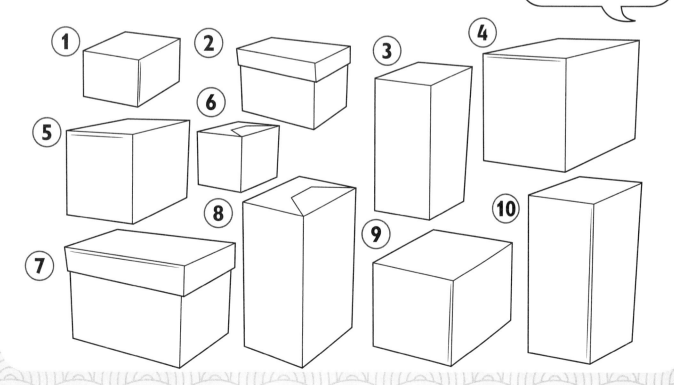

**1** 23 CD4 Listen and draw lines. There is one example.

Alex          Dan          Grace          Hugo

May          Bill          Sue

## 2 🔍✏️ Follow the lines and write.

| ~~bedroom~~ living room kitchen hallway |

① ② ③ ④

_bedroom_ _____ _____ _____

## 3 ✏️ Draw your house.

**Me!**

My house has

_____
_____
_____
_____
_____
_____
_____ .

**4** 🔊 **28** ✏️ Listen and color the stars.

**5** 🔍 ✏️ Match and write.

① She's drawing a _____picture_____ .

② He's reading a _____ .

③ She's sitting on a _____ .

④ They're listening to _____ .

⑤ He's driving a _____ .

⑥ They're playing _____ .

chair

tennis

car

book

music

picture

**6** 🔍✏️ Look, read, and write.

Where are the children?          in the _____kitchen_____

How many people are there?          _____two_____

**1** What's the girl eating?          some _____

**2** What does the boy have?          a _____

**3** What's the girl doing?          listening to _____

**4** What animal can the boy see?     an _____

**5** Who's pointing?          the _____

**7** 🎧32 CD4 ✏️ Listen and circle the "h" words.

① ② ③ ④

⑤ ⑥ ⑦ ⑧ ⑨

**8** ✏️ Complete the sentences.

| eating | ~~listening~~ | reading | taking |

① He's ___listening___ to music.  ② She's _____ a bath.

③ He's _____ a fish.  ④ She's _____ a book.

# My picture dictionary

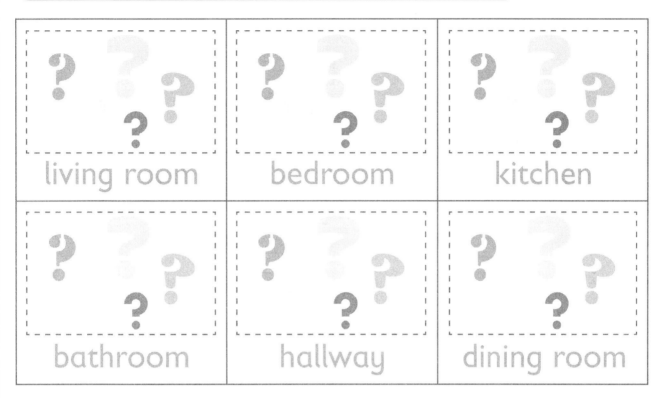

| | | |
|---|---|---|
| living room | bedroom | kitchen |
| bathroom | hallway | dining room |

# My star card

 Can you say these words?

Color the stars.

**1** 🎵37 CD4 ✏️ Listen and color.

**2** ✏️ Circle and write the words.

| | | | | | | | | |
|---|---|---|---|---|---|---|---|---|
| a | w | e | i | f | i | s | h | s |
| c | h | o | c | o | l | a | t | e |
| a | b | r | e | c | k | f | a | m |
| k | l | t | c | h | e | j | p | r |
| e | b | u | r | g | e | r | p | o |
| p | r | o | e | v | i | s | l | b |
| b | a | n | a | n | a | t | e | g |
| j | z | o | m | e | r | s | t | u |
| o | r | a | n | g | e | v | i | e |

1  _____

2  _____

3  _____

4 _____

5 _____

6  ice cream

7  _____

8  _____

**3**  Write the words.

1. → _cat_

2. →

3. →

4. →

**4** Read and complete.

| young |
| ~~eating~~ |
| banana |
| cake |

The small monkey's ___eating___ an orange, and the big monkey has some _____ . The old monkey's eating a _____ , and the _____ monkey has ice cream.

**5** 🔊 42 CD4 ✏️ Listen and check (✓) or put an ✗.

1.  ☐ ✓   ☐   ☐   ☐

2.  ☐   ☐   ☐   ☐

3.  ☐   ☐   ☐   ☐

4.  ☐   ☐   ☐   ☐

**6** ✏️ Write "like" or "don't like."

Me! I _____ fish.

Me! I _____ burgers.

Me! I _____ ice cream.

Me! I _____ apples.

Listen and color. There is one example.

**8**  **Listen and write the words.**

| bike | white | drive | nine | ~~like~~ | five |
|------|-------|-------|------|----------|------|

①

② **5**

③

_like_

④ **9**

⑤

⑥

**9** **Check (✓) the boxes.**

| Name | 🍎🍎 | 🍌 | | | | |
|------|------|-----|---|---|---|---|
| Me | | | | | | |
| | | | | | | |
| | | | | | | |
| | | | | | | |

**Now ask and answer in groups.**

Do you like apples?      Yes, I do.

88

# My picture dictionary

apple

banana

burger

cake

chocolate

ice cream

# My star card

 Can you say these words?

Color the stars.

**1**  Read and circle a word.

This is Fred Food.

His nose is a banana / an ice-cream cone.

His mouth is a fish / a burger.

His ears are apples / oranges.

His hair is grapes / kiwis.

His eyes are cakes / burgers.

Now you! **2**  Draw and color your Fred Food.

Fred Food

**3** 🔍✏️ Order the pictures.

①

② 

③ 

**4** 🔍✏️ Read and write.

| brushing   washing   washing |
|---|

He's _____ his hands.

She's _____ her teeth.

He's _____ his apples.

9 10 11 12

**1** Check (✓) a box.

|  |  |  |  |  |  |  |
|---|---|---|---|---|---|---|
| reading a book |  |  |  |  |  |  |
| eating fish |  |  |  |  |  |  |
| watching TV |  |  |  |  |  |  |
| taking a bath |  |  |  |  |  |  |

Now ask and answer. Check (✓) your friend's box.

What's the old monster doing?    He's eating fish.

|  |  |  |  |  |  |  |
|---|---|---|---|---|---|---|
| reading a book |  |  |  |  |  |  |
| eating fish |  |  |  |  |  |  |
| watching TV |  |  |  |  |  |  |
| taking a bath |  |  |  |  |  |  |

## 2 🖊 Circle the different word.

1. kiwi      apple      orange      (guitar)

2. truck      ice cream      train      bus

3. burger      tiger      giraffe      crocodile

4. bathroom      kitchen      bedroom      chocolate

5. motorcycle      helicopter      truck      hallway

6. play      swim      bike      ride

## 3 🔍🖊 Read and complete. Draw.

I'm _____ .

I'm at home in
the  kitchen. I like

_____ ,

but I don't like

_____ .

My favorite food is

_____ .

Me!

93

# Grammar reference

**1** Order the words.

1 ( your ) ( name? ) ( What's ) _____

2 ( old ) ( are ) ( you? ) ( How ) _____

**2** Look and complete.

| He's She's He's She's |
|---|

1 _____ Scott. _____ six.

2 _____ Sally. _____ seven.

**3** Look and complete.

| Is Is is isn't |
|---|

1 _____ your ball in your car?     Yes, it _____ .

2 _____ your ball on the table?     No, it _____ .

**4** Circle the sentences.

Wearen'tsad.We'rehappy.Arewebeautiful?

**5** **Look and complete.**

It's   They're

(1) Look at the dog. _____ long.

(2) Look at the two cats. _____ small.

 **6** **Order the words.**

(1) ( face. )( have )( I )( a clean ) _____

(2) ( You )( short hair. )( have ) _____

 **7** **Circle the sentences.**

Theyhavetails.Theydon'thavehair.Dotheyhavelegs?

**8** **Look and complete.**

doesn't have   has

(1) ✓ He _____ your red pants.

(2) ✗ He _____ your red pants.

**9** Order the words.

① can · sing. · He · _____

② They · swim. · can't · _____

③ Can · ride a bike? · you · _____

**10** Look and complete.

| am | not | Are | Are |

① _____ you flying your plane? Yes, I _____ .

② _____ you playing the guitar? No, I'm _____ .

**11** Circle the sentences.

What'shedoing?Heistakingabath.Ishereading?

**12** Look and complete.

| like | don't like |

① 🙂 I _____ cake.

② 🙁 I _____ ice cream.

# About me

School: _____

Grade: _____

Write "hi" in your language(s).

# My language skills

Match the pictures.

# I can ... # Units 1-3

Color the face: I can do it!

1  Listen and point.

1  2  3  4  5
6  7  8  9  10

1

2 Say the words.

2

3 Read and match.

3      4      5      6

3

4 Write.

My name's _____ .

I'm _____ years old.

4

# I can ...

## Units 4-6

| | Color the face: I can do it! |
|---|---|

1  Listen and point.

2 Say the words.

3 Read and draw.

| | |
|---|---|
| A small fish | A big fish |

4 Write the words.

eyes
ears
nose
mouth

# I can ...  Units 7-9

**1**  Listen and point.

**2** Say the words.

**3** Read and color.

She has a yellow
T-shirt and a blue skirt.

He has a green
T-shirt and red pants.

**4** Write what you can do.

I can _____ .

| Color the face: I can do it! |
| --- |
| 1 ☺ |
| 2 ☺ |
| 3 ☺ |
| 4 ☺ |

# I can ...          Units 10–12

| | Color the face: I can do it! |
|---|---|

**1**  Listen and point. What are they doing?

| 1 | ☺ |
|---|---|

**2** 💬 Say the words.

| 2 | ☺ |
|---|---|

**3** 🔍 Read and draw.

She's eating ice cream.

He's eating an apple.

| 3 | ☺ |
|---|---|

**4** ✏️ Write three foods you like.

I like _____ , _____ , and _____ .

| 4 | ☺ |
|---|---|

103

# English and me

Color the face. English is:

 OK

 Good

 Great

 Fantastic

An English song I can sing:

_____

An English book I can read:

_____

English words I know:

Wow!

_____

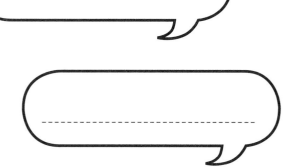

_____

_____

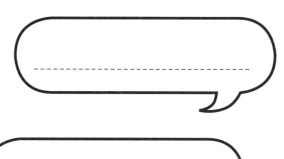

_____

# My classroom

Draw a picture of your classroom.

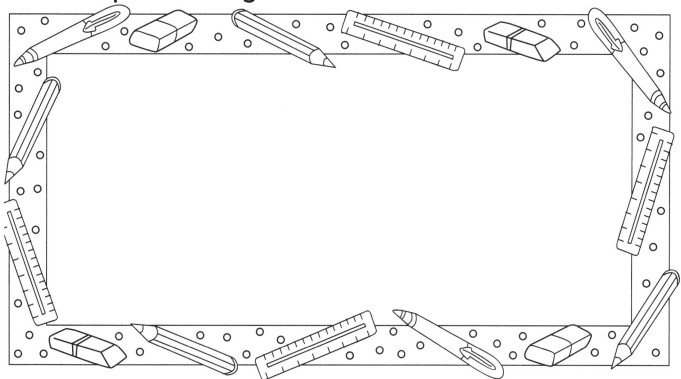

Now draw your school things.

|  |  |
|---|---|
| My bag. | My table. |
| My pencil case. | My eraser. |

# About me

Draw or stick pictures of your favorite things.

My favorite number.

My favorite color.

My favorite toy.

My favorite animal.

# My pet

Draw a picture of your favorite pet.

Animal: _____

Name: _____

Color: _____

# Fun time

Draw a picture of something you like doing.

Answer the questions. Check (✓) the boxes.
Can you …

| | | |
|---|---|---|
| … play soccer? | Yes ☐ | No ☐ |
| … swim? | Yes ☐ | No ☐ |
| … play the guitar? | Yes ☐ | No ☐ |
| … ride a bike? | Yes ☐ | No ☐ |
| … play tennis? | Yes ☐ | No ☐ |

# My house

Draw a picture or stick a photograph of your house.

## Check (✓) the boxes.

My house is                                    big ☐ small ☐

My house has  a kitchen ☐ a living room ☐ a hallway ☐

a dining room ☐ a bathroom ☐ bedrooms ☐

How many bedrooms are there?        1 ☐ 2 ☐ 3 ☐

4 ☐ More! ☐

# Food

Draw or stick pictures of food. Can you write the food words?

I like ... 🙂

I don't like ... 🙁

# Thanks and Acknowledgments

## Authors' thanks

Many thanks to everyone at Cambridge University Press and in particular to:

Rosemary Bradley for supervising the whole project and for her keen editorial eye;
Emily Hird for her energy, enthusiasm, and enormous organizational capacity;
Colin Sage for his hard work, good ideas, and helpful suggestions;
Claire Appleyard for her editorial contribution.

Many thanks to Karen Elliot for her expertise and enthusiasm in the writing of the Phonics sections.

We would also like to thank all our pupils and colleagues at Star English, El Palmar, Murcia, and especially Jim Kelly and Julie Woodman for their help and suggestions at various stages of the project.

## Dedications

I would like to dedicate this book to the women who have been my pillars of strength: Milagros Marín, Sara de Alba, Elia Navarro, and Maricarmen Balsalobre - CN

To Paloma, for her love, encouragement, and unwavering support. Thanks. - MT

**The Authors and Publishers would like to thank the following teachers for their help in reviewing the material and for the invaluable feedback they provided:**

Luciana Pittondo, Soledad Gimenez, Argentina; Gan Ping, Zou Yang, China; Keily Duran, Colombia; Elvia Gutierrez Reyes, Yadira Hernandez, Mexico; Rachel Lunan, Russia; Lorraine Mealing, Sharon Hopkins, Spain; Inci Kartal, Turkey.

**The authors and publishers would like to thank the following consultants for their invaluable feedback:**

Coralyn Bradshaw, Pippa Mayfield, Hilary Ratcliff, Melanie Williams.

**We would also like to thank all the teachers who allowed us to observe their classes and who gave up their invaluable time for interviews and focus groups.**

## The authors and publishers are grateful to the following illustrators:

A. Corazon Abierto, c/o Syvlie Poggio; John Batten, c/o Beehive; Beatrice Costamagna, c/o Pickled ink; James Elston, c/o Syvlie Poggio; Chris Garbutt, c/o Arena; Lucía Serrano Guerroro; Andrew Hennessey; Kelly Kennedy, c/o Syvlie Poggio; Rob McKlurkan, c/o The Bright Agency; Melanie Sharp, c/o Syvlie Poggio; Marie Simpson, c/o Pickled ink; Emily Skinner, c/o Graham-Cameron Illustration; Lisa Smith; Gary Swift; Matt Ward, c/o Beehive; Lisa Williams, c/o Syvlie Poggio

## The publishers are grateful to the following contributors:

Wild Apple Design Ltd: page design
Blooberry: additional design
Lon Chan: cover design
Melanie Sharp: cover illustration
John Green and Tim Woolf, TEFL Audio: audio recordings
John Marshall Media, Inc. and Lisa Hutchins: audio recordings for the American English edition
Robert Lee: song writing
hyphen S.A.: publishing management, American English edition

**Hi!** (page 9)

 **My school** (page 15)

 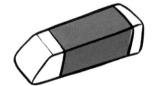 

 **Favorite toys** (page 23)